THE WORKBOOK

Why America Needs to Repent

DWANE MASSENBURG

WESTBOW
PRESS®
A DIVISION OF THOMAS NELSON
& ZONDERVAN

WestBow Press books may be ordered through booksellers or by contacting:

WestBow Press
A Division of Thomas Nelson & Zondervan
1663 Liberty Drive
Bloomington, IN 47403
www.westbowpress.com
844-714-3454

Scripture taken from the King James Version of the Bible.

Scripture taken from the New King James Version® Copyright © 1982 by Thomas Nelson. Used by permission. All rights reserved.

ISBN: 978-1-6642-6362-8 (sc)
ISBN: 978-1-6642-6363-5 (e)

Print information available on the last page.

WestBow Press rev. date: 04/22/2022

Study to shew thyself approved unto God, a workman that needeth not to be ashamed, rightly dividing the word of truth. (2 Timothy 2:15 KJV).

Acknowledgments

I would like to thank Associate Pastor Jacquelyn B. Jones. God has plans for people to come into your life according to His will. I am in awe of how God placed and then replaced you in my life a second time so this work could be completed. Thank you for allowing God to use you. Thank you for pondering, studying, thinking, and writing the questions in this workbook which invite people to consider repentance before God. You have fulfilled a very worthy task.

I would like to thank my wife Sophia Massenburg for once again providing me the love, time, and space to get this work accomplished. God bless you and your spiritual gift of "helps". This work would not exist without you. I praise God for the lives we may touch by this work. I praise God for using us as a couple to assist in spreading His gospel. You are appreciated.

Preface

First, I would like to say congratulations to anybody who is reading these words. If you are reading these words, more than likely that means that you have purchased and are already starting to read the book "Why America Needs to Repent". The fact that you are now looking at this workbook means that you are no longer just a casual observer, but you are a student of the Bible. You are a theologian working out your salvation with God.

> "Wherefore, my beloved, as ye have always obeyed, not as in my presence only, but now much more in my absence, work out your own salvation with fear and trembling. For it is God which worketh in you both to will and to do of his good pleasure." (Philippians 2:12-13 KJV).

So, keep on my brothers and sisters. Keep on working it out and never doubt that God is with you. God is on your side, and he wants you to win.

Secondly, as a Pastor, I would like to assure you that you are heading in the right direction. You are walking in the light.

> "He who believes in Him is not condemned; but he who does not believe is condemned already, because he has not believed in the name of the only begotten Son of God. And this is the condemnation, that the light has come into the world, and men loved darkness rather than light, because their deeds were evil. For everyone practicing evil hates the light and does not come to the light, lest his deeds should be exposed. But he who does the truth comes to the light, that his deeds may be clearly seen, that they have been done in God." (John 3:18-21 NKJV).

So, keep walking my brothers and sisters in Christ. Keep reading. Keep studying. Keep praying. Keep asking. Stay in the fellowship. There is no such thing as a finish line to Christianity. As long as we live on this side of death, we will always be a work in progress. We never arrive at Christianity.

This workbook and the accompanying book are designed for conversation. Each chapter deserves a pause. Find your agreement or disagreement with the chapter in the Word of God. I pray that you have good conversations with your family or church congregation. Reason together and let God chart your course.

Introduction

Why America Needs to Repent for the Kingdom of God is at Hand

"He that is not with me is against me: and he that gathereth not with me scattereth. When the unclean spirit is gone out of a man, he walketh through dry places, seeking rest; and finding none, he saith, I will return unto my house whence I came out. And when he cometh, he findeth it swept and garnished. Then goeth he, and taketh to him seven other spirits more wicked than himself; and they enter in, and dwell there: and the last state of that man is worse than the first." (Luke 11:23-26 KJV).

Those of us that claim our redemption through Jesus Christ are the children of God. We are a "chosen generation, a royal priesthood, a holy nation, and a peculiar people." (1 Peter 2:9 KJV). We are joint heirs of everything God has for us as a result of his blood on the cross. We are forgiven.

Yet, with all of those blessings, our behavior requires repentance. Since the fall of Adam and Eve, there are many temptations that we still fall for today. Satan continues to entice us. We all have weaknesses that are contrary to the will of God because we still live in this flesh. How do we get to the point, on a daily basis, wherein we disobey the word of our Creator? What is in our DNA (deoxyribonucleic acid), that causes us to rebel? Have we lost our fear of God? Have we forgotten the glory of God?

> "The fear of the Lord is the beginning of wisdom: and the knowledge of the holy is understanding." (Proverbs 9:10 KJV).

The fear here is referring to reverence for God. It is describing what the New Testament refers to as "Abba Father". This affectionate term is like a child staring up and adoring their loving parent. The child has complete trust in everything the parent says and does. The child is totally dependent and seeks acceptance and approval from their parent. This is how we should reverence God throughout our entire life because no matter how old we may get; our age is insignificant relative to God. God's desire is for our relationship to continue as one of reverence for Him as we abide in Him. However, we all have a choice to follow the path of sin or righteousness.

Our Path to Sin or Righteousness - Lessons from the Life of Judas

Why Judas?

Many self-righteous Christians may claim that they are not as bad as Judas. We think to ourselves, "I would never do what Judas did." Judas Iscariot had a personal relationship with Jesus for around three years. He walked with Jesus. He had intimate, personal conversations with Christ. He most likely was present for many of the miracles of Christ. Yet, he turned Jesus over to the chief priests and elders for thirty pieces of silver. Thirty pieces of silver are all it took for Judas to betray their personal bond. Judas turned his back on Jesus and at the same time, he betrayed the comradery amongst all of the disciples. Truthfully though, Judas was not that much different from all of us.

> "When the morning was come, all the chief priests and elders of the people took counsel against Jesus to put him to death: and when they had bound him, they led him away, and delivered him to Pontius Pilate the governor. Then Judas, which had betrayed him, when he saw that he was condemned, repented himself, and brought again the thirty pieces of silver to the chief priests and elders, saying, I have sinned in that I have betrayed the innocent blood. And they said, what is that to us? see thou to that. And he cast down the pieces of silver in the temple, and departed, and went and hanged himself." (Matthew 27:1-5 KJV).

In spite of what Judas did, he was not the only wayward Jew in and around Jerusalem at the time. The religious leaders, in the community, absolutely let Jesus down. Unlike our society in America today, most people that lived during that time could not read. The chief priest, elders, and scribes were the most educated people. They had studied the prophets. Yet, they refused to accept that Jesus Christ was the Son of God.

Secondly, the masses in Jerusalem for the Passover feast must have heard about all of the miracles and wisdom Jesus shared. There were obviously many people in the crowd He had helped which is why they sang His praises as He entered Jerusalem for the last time.

> "And a very great multitude spread their garments in the way; others cut down branches from the trees, and strawed them in the way. And the multitudes that went before, and that followed, cried, saying, Hosanna to the son of David: Blessed

is he that cometh in the name of the Lord; Hosanna in the highest." (Matthew 21:8-9 KJV).

Yet, they did nothing to stop the crucifixion. The good works Jesus had done were not enough for anyone to stand up to those that wanted to crucify him. One could say that the welcoming crowd allowed Jesus to die. They cried out to save the murderer, Barabbas instead of Jesus. All of those Jesus had helped must have been too fearful for their own lives to stop this miscarriage of justice. Where are we when injustice is occurring?

Lastly, it was not just Judas but all of the disciples that scattered in fear when Jesus was captured. (John 16:32, Mark 14:50). They left the mentor that had been walking with them and training them for more than three years.

We could use any of these people or all of these people as examples of those that need to repent. Therefore, Judas is a worthy candidate to use for our analysis on who should repent. The truth is Judas is no worse than anyone else. For a moment in time, it appears that Judas was only thinking about himself. Most of us can identify with moments of being self-absorbed. In that respect, we are all like Judas. We have all sold our relationship to our Savior for money, riches, fame, sex, power, and anything else that pleases our ego and our flesh. In fact, most people dishonor their relationship with God at least weekly, if not daily. An honest look in the mirror will reveal how much we are like Judas.

Reckless

There are times when all of us have been in the presence of someone we respect, honor, and revere. When we are in the presence of these highly esteemed people, we normally humble ourselves. Oftentimes, even to our own detriment sometimes, we may give too much respect and leeway to a coach, supervisor, or pastor. No matter how old we get, most people hold their parents in high esteem and thus have a tendency to be very respectful to them throughout their lives. We follow their words, listen to what they say, and perhaps try to mimic what they do. When something comes up that we do not understand we may ask them about it for clarity. Most, usually do not ask about it in arrogant pride. Even when a brand-new subject comes up, the tendency is to give the highly respected person some latitude concerning their knowledge on the subject. However, Judas seemed to be reckless and proud in his dealings with Jesus.

"Then Jesus six days before the Passover came to Bethany, where Lazarus was, which had been dead, whom he raised from the dead. There they made him a supper; and Martha served: but Lazarus was one of them that sat at the table with him. Then took Mary a pound of ointment of spikenard, very costly, and anointed the feet of Jesus, and wiped his feet with her hair: and the house was filled with the odour of the ointment. Then saith one of his disciples, Judas Iscariot, Simon's son, which should betray him, "Why was not this ointment sold for three hundred pence, and given to the poor?" This he said, not that he cared for the poor; but because he was a thief, and had the bag, and bare what was put therein." (John 12:1-6 KJV).

How could Judas still question anything Jesus did or allowed after the years of walking, talking, and watching Him perform miracles? Judas was reckless in thinking that he had wisdom that was superior. The miracles were so great, he must have known Jesus was not an ordinary man. Judas once again shows his recklessness during the last supper.

"And he said, Go into the city to such a man, and say unto him, The Master saith, My time is at hand; I will keep the passover at thy house with my disciples. And the disciples did as Jesus had appointed them; and they made ready the Passover. Now when the even was come, he sat down with the twelve. And as they did eat, he said, Verily I say unto you, that one of you shall betray me. And they were exceeding sorrowful, and began every one of them to say unto him, Lord, is it I? And he answered and said, He that dippeth his hand with me in the dish, the same shall betray me. The Son of man goeth as it is written of him: but woe unto that man by whom the Son of man is betrayed! it had been good for that man if he had not been born. Then Judas, which betrayed him, answered and said, Master, is it I? He said unto him, Thou hast said." (Matthew 26:18-25 KJV).

Here, Judas' arrogance shows up as he asks, "Is it I?" He knew very well what he was planning to do. Judas was just ignoring the presence and power of Jesus by asking this question. He was being reckless.

Being reckless is an issue for all of us. People often say I did not know about a certain thing. That may be true about some things but there are many things we do know. Yet, even knowing things we should not do, we act just like Judas and do them anyway. Living reckless, we snub our finger at Almighty God. In essence, we let God know that he is not important enough for us to heed His words.

Realization

The next stage in a sinful life is when we first realize that our sin is recognized. One day our recklessness against the word, the will, and the way of God will lead to a reckoning moment. It is a moment similar to seeing the windshield shatter when you know your parents told you not to throw the ball towards the driveway. It is that moment when the cookie jar slides off the counter and breaks when your mother told you to leave the cookies alone in the first place. It is that moment when the "other" woman tells you she is pregnant with your child after having an affair. It is the moment when Satan's trap has sprung and there is no turning back. In Judas' case, the moment of realization came when Pilate got involved.

> "When the morning was come, all the chief priests and elders of the people took counsel against Jesus to put him to death. And when they had bound him, they led him away, and delivered him to Pontius Pilate the governor." (Matthew 27:1-2 KJV).

Judas was caught. Many Bible scholars believe that perhaps Judas was thinking that Jesus would have to start a revolt, take over and become king of a new country if he forced Jesus to take a stand. Unfortunately, Judas' scheme did not work because that was not the plan of God. Judas was counting on Jesus' confinement to only be an issue for the Jews to handle. However, everything changed when the Jewish religious leaders delivered Jesus to Pontius Pilate. Pilate was a Roman and he had the power to sentence someone to death. It was at this point Judas realized that he had done something much larger than perhaps he had anticipated.

So, it is with us when we sin. For a while, we may not realize that we are going to get caught playing with fire. Then the door slams and we find ourselves in the middle of a mess. The fire is hot in our hands and our clothes. We cannot shake it off.

Remorse and Return

When many people are caught in sin their first reaction may not be remorse for the sin. Their first reaction may be remorse for getting caught. In Matthew 27:3 the text says Judas repented and tried to return the thirty pieces of silver. He was trying to make it right. He was trying to fix the situation. He was trying to make it go away. He was trying to bargain.

So often, many in society try to do the same thing that Judas tried. We try to glue the cookie jar back together. People put on makeup to hide physical abuse. They go to get an abortion to rid themselves of an adulterous pregnancy. Some will tell a chain of lies attempting to get out of a sin that was committed. Some will make every attempt to hide evidence. A person at this stage is still thinking like Satan. They are only doing and saying things for selfish reasons in order to escape the repercussions of their sin being discovered.

Regret and True Repentance

When there is nothing between us and time, we come face to face with what has been done. Finally, in Matthew 27:4, after the elders, chief priest and scribes, told Judas there would be no opportunity to buy back whom he had betrayed, Judas knew his plight was sealed. Now he was forced to think not only about getting caught and the personal embarrassment he would suffer. Suddenly, regret for what he did to Jesus was real.

Finally, Judas demonstrates a true picture of what it is like to have a repentant heart. When he throws down the thirty pieces of silver that he bargained for, he demonstrates a total relinquishment of everything worldly. All of his selfishness is gone. The weight of what he has done in committing the worse crime (depending on how you look at it since it was a part of God's plan for Christian salvation) since Adam and Eve betrayed God in the Garden of Eden, is now squarely upon the shoulders of Judas. He now knows he cannot shrink away from it. It is done.

True repentance for us should look the same way. When the judge has delivered the sentence and a person spends their first nights in prison, perhaps now the convicted felon can reflect on how he or she got involved in the situation that led them there. Perhaps there is time to reflect on who and how many people were hurt because of their crime. Now, there is time to reflect on the pain caused. This is true regret. As the nights go by behind bars perhaps now true repentance can take place before God as the convicted felon admits they went down the wrong path. They would take it back if they could because of what happened to the victim. They would never do it again. Repentance is when your heart, mind, and soul say, "never again", for the sake of others and for the sake of everyone else that suffers a negative impact from the situation. True repentance is not just being sorry for selfish reasons. True repentance is regret and turning away from something for the sake of others and honoring the righteousness of God.

Our Opportunities

Judas threw down the thirty pieces of silver when it was too late. Suppose he had given up his plan and hit his knees in repentance when he was at the "last supper" with Jesus and asked, "Is it

I?" Suppose he had given up his plans just before he met with the chief priest and elders. Suppose Judas had stopped on the way to the Garden of Gethsemane, with the soldiers behind him, and said, "I cannot do this".

Daily we have opportunities to continue or stop on our path to sin or righteousness. The opportunity to repent is available at all times. No, we cannot blame everything on Adam and Eve. Yes, we are born physically with a sinful nature because of Adam and Eve. However, because of the blood of Jesus on the cross, when we accept Him, the Holy Spirit enters inside of us. Our sinful nature is no longer in charge unless we allow it to be. The Spirit begins to allow us to recognize sin as we live our lives. Now, we have a choice each day. (Read Romans 6-8). The best life God has planned for us includes repentance. Not being serious about repentance only leads to more trouble.

> "He that is not with me is against me: and he that gathereth not with me scattereth. When the unclean spirit is gone out of a man, he walketh through dry places, seeking rest; and finding none, he saith, I will return unto my house whence I came out. And when he cometh, he findeth it swept and garnished. Then goeth he, and taketh to him seven other spirits more wicked than himself; and they enter in, and dwell there: and the last state of that man is worse than the first." (Luke 11:23-26 KJV).

Our opportunity is to repent now. Our opportunity is to repent daily. Our opportunity is to be proactive in resisting sin instead of being reactive when the harvest from our sins is already causing corruption in our lives.

Chapter 1

AMERICA

Why America Needs to Repent for the Kingdom of God is at Hand

"America is not a perfect place to live. The perfect place has not existed since Adam and Eve were in the Garden of Eden."

1. What are the signs that Christians in America are under the divine judgment of God at this time in history?

_____

_____

_____

_____

2. What is repentance and how does it help us as Christians?

_____

_____

_____

_____

3. Has history taught us anything about how God deals with a sinful nation?

_____

_____

_____

_____

4. Why does America need to repent?

_____

_____

_____

_____

5. How is America out of balance when we compare ourselves with the practice of God's word?

_____

_____

_____

_____

6. What is the mark of a true Christian?

_____

_____

_____

_____

7. What are some signs of a sinful lifestyle as seen in society today that were not so readily seen thirty years ago?

_____

_____

_____

_____

8. How has the government contributed to the demise of Christianity in America?

_____

_____

_____

_____

9. Is simply asking God to forgive you for your sins the same as repentance? Why or why not?

_____

_____

_____

_____

10. How did God deal with Israel, His chosen people when they refused to repent?

_____

_____

_____

_____

11. How do we know God is constantly trying to reach humanity?

_____

_____

_____

_____

12. Why is the life of the Apostle Paul a great example of repentance?

_____

_____

_____

_____

13. How is it possible for America to have a perfect union?

_____

_____

_____

_____

14. How has the moral character of Americans weakened?

_____

_____

_____

_____

15. If Christianity is the most prevalent religion in America, should Christians take responsibility for the moral decay of this country? Why?

_____

_____

_____

_____

Chapter 2 – I Repent for

NOT CARING ENOUGH TO READ THE BIBLE

Why America Needs to Repent for the Kingdom of God is at Hand

"Everyone should have some type of realization that God's word is the most important thing He has blessed us to have in our generation."

1. What drove you to study this book?

   _____

   _____

   _____

   _____

2. What did you know about repentance before embarking upon this study?

   _____

   _____

   _____

3. What do you hope to learn about repentance?

   _____

   _____

   _____

   _____

4. How important is it to you for you to know God's word?

_____

_____

_____

_____

5. What are some things that distract us from studying God's word?

_____

_____

_____

_____

6. After studying this chapter, what am I going to do differently?

_____

_____

_____

_____

Chapter 3 – I Repent for

BEING COVETOUS

Why America Needs to Repent for the Kingdom of God is at Hand

"Let your conversation be without covetousness; and be content with such things as ye have: for he hath said, I will never leave thee, nor forsake thee. So that we may boldly say, The Lord is my helper, and I will not fear what man shall do unto me."
(Hebrews 13:5-6 KJV)

1. What does it mean to be covetous?

   _____

   _____

   _____

   _____

2. List five commandments included in the *Ten Commandments* directed towards the behavior of humankind.

   _____

   _____

   _____

   _____

3. What are some ways we covet that are not pleasing to God?

_____

_____

_____

_____

4. How do jealousy, pride, envy, entitlement, and selfishness play a part in covetousness?

_____

_____

_____

_____

5. What are some long-term effects of covetousness?

_____

_____

_____

_____

6. After studying this chapter, what are you going to do differently?

_____

_____

_____

_____

Chapter 4 – I Repent for

NOT PRACTICING TRUE LOVE

Why America Needs to Repent for the Kingdom of God is at Hand

"True love is not what one gets; neither should it be graded by what is demanded. God has freely shown us, love"

1. How did God freely demonstrate His love toward us?

_____

_____

_____

_____

2. How can we show love in our everyday life?

_____

_____

_____

_____

3. We should show love regardless of the situation. What is a Biblical example of how Jesus showed love in a difficult situation?

_____

_____

_____

_____

4. What does the statement, "Love can be hard" mean to you?

_____

_____

_____

_____

5. Is unconditional love and true love the same? Explain why or why not.

_____

_____

_____

_____

6. List five Bible verses that demonstrate God's love for us.

_____

_____

_____

_____

7. After studying this chapter, what am I going to do differently?

_____

_____

_____

_____

Chapter 5 – I Repent for
NOT WATCHING

Why America Needs to Repent for the Kingdom of God is at Hand

"Watching does not mean worry. God is taking care of everything. He blesses us. He provides for us. He protects us. He loves us. Watching is an awareness. Watching is being prepared."

1. How does watching apply to the Christian life?

    _____

    _____

    _____

    _____

2. How does 1 Corinthians 12:10 give us the ability to practice Christian watching.

    _____

    _____

    _____

    _____

3. How do Christians know what things they should be watching for?

    _____

    _____

    _____

    _____

4. Should Christians be watching for the return of Jesus? If so, what should they expect?

_____

_____

_____

_____

5. How does one prepare himself/herself for the return of Jesus?

_____

_____

_____

_____

6. After studying this chapter, what am I going to do differently?

_____

_____

_____

_____

Chapter 6 – I Repent for

ACTING LIKE THERE ARE ALTERNATIVES TO GOD

Why America Needs to Repent for the Kingdom of God is at Hand

"For there are three that bear witness in heaven: the Father, the Word, and the Holy Spirit; and these three are one. And there are three that bear witness on earth: The Spirit, the water, and the blood; and these three agree as one. (1 John 5:7-8 KJV)."

1. What are the more persistent areas of unbelief you have seen in your walk with Christ?

    _____

    _____

    _____

    _____

2. God has given us many blessings. Which ones have we made an alternative to God?

    _____

    _____

    _____

    _____

3. Why do the atheist and agnostics call the Christian a hypocrite?

    _____

    _____

    _____

    _____

4. Read the Book of Job, chapters 38 through 41, and give your observation.

    _____

    _____

    _____

    _____

5. After studying this chapter, what am I going to do differently?

    _____

    _____

    _____

    _____

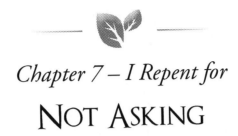

Chapter 7 – I Repent for

NOT ASKING

Why America Needs to Repent for the Kingdom of God is at Hand

"Jesus himself demonstrated that He does not make demands of God the father. In the garden of Gethsemane Jesus wanted God the Father's will to be done."

1. What does God's Word say to us about making requests of the Lord?

_____

_____

_____

_____

2. What are the conditions tied to God's promise to give us whatsoever we ask of Him?

_____

_____

_____

_____

3. What are some things we should not ask of God?

_____

_____

_____

_____

4. Why do we fail to ask God for help when we need it?

_____

_____

_____

_____

5. Should we continue to ask God if He does not answer our prayer requests? Why or why not?

_____

_____

_____

_____

6. Should we go to God for even the small things we need?

_____

_____

_____

7. If God knows what we need, why do we have to ask Him?

_____

_____

_____

8. What does it mean to ask, according to God's will?

_____

_____

_____

9. After studying this chapter, what am I going to do differently?

_____

_____

_____

_____

Chapter 8 – I Repent for
NOT ACKNOWLEDGING THE FRUITS OF THE SPIRIT

Why America Needs to Repent for the Kingdom of God is at Hand

"The fruits of the Spirit are diverse but they are the same. They all show love and reverence to God and love for fellow human beings. Some of the fruit may not be as developed as others, but; the Holy Spirit in us is working on that. All of the fruit has the same purpose."

1. How does the Holy Spirit work in our lives through the fruits of the Spirit?

_____

_____

_____

_____

2. Explain this statement, "The fruits of the Spirit are diverse, but they are the same."

_____

_____

_____

_____

3. What are the nine fruits of the Spirit and where are they found in the scripture?

    _____

    _____

    _____

    _____

4. What is the evidence of the Holy Spirit in our lives?

    _____

    _____

    _____

    _____

5. How did Jesus reference the fruit of the Spirit?

    _____

    _____

    _____

    _____

6. After studying this chapter, what am I going to do differently?

    _____

    _____

    _____

    _____

Chapter 9 – I Repent for

BEING SO SELFISH I FORGET THE PLIGHT OF THE POOR

Why America Needs to Repent for the Kingdom of God is at Hand

"It is not enough just to realize the poor are there. They should not be ignored. Christians are actually, called to do something about it. Our society says, get more, take more, and go more, when some among us are just trying to find some food to eat tonight."

1. Why should we be attentive and responsive to the needs and hurts of other people?

    _____

    _____

    _____

    _____

2. What does the Bible say about helping the poor?

    _____

    _____

    _____

    _____

3. Proverbs 14:31 talks about why we should be concerned about the plight of the poor. How do you think God feels when we neglect the poor?

_____

_____

_____

_____

4. Why has God given each of us the ability to make a difference in the life of the poor?

_____

_____

_____

_____

5. After studying this chapter, what am I going to do differently?

_____

_____

_____

_____

Chapter 10 – I Repent for

USING GOD LIKE A VENDING MACHINE

Why America Needs to Repent for the Kingdom of God is at Hand

"Any good vending machine will have a selection to choose from. Some seem to act like God should be on standby with financial blessings, a good spouse, successful children, and good health."

1. How would you explain God to a child who asked, "Who is God and why does He exist?"

    _____

    _____

    _____

    _____

2. How can we be conscious of God's presence in our life?

    _____

    _____

    _____

    _____

3. Why is it that most people can only experience God when He is answering their prayers and granting their wishes?

    _____

    _____

    _____

    _____

4. After studying this chapter, what am I going to do differently?

_____

_____

_____

_____

Chapter 11 – I Repent for

MISUSING AND ABUSING MY FELLOW MAN AND FELLOW WOMAN

Why America Needs to Repent for the Kingdom of God is at Hand

"Treating people, the way you want to be treated seems like it would almost be a natural thing to do. It seems like it would be an easy roadmap concerning how one would handle business and daily transactions. Yet the world is full of people inappropriately using people."

1. What does the "Golden Rule" mean to you and how does one live out this rule in their daily life?

   _____

   _____

   _____

   _____

2. What Biblical scriptures support the use of the Golden Rule?

   _____

   _____

   _____

   _____

3. Does Matthew 7:12 teach us how to handle the abuse of women and men? Explain!

_____

_____

_____

_____

4. How did God instruct the Israelites to care for others?

_____

_____

_____

_____

5. What is the most common reason people misuse and abuse others?

_____

_____

_____

_____

6. How does God hold us accountable when we misuse other people?

_____

_____

_____

_____

7. How do people use people who have fallen into poverty to make a profit?

_____

_____

_____

_____

8. After studying this chapter, what am I going to do differently?

_____

_____

_____

_____

Chapter 12 – I Repent for

ALLOWING RACISM TO CONTINUE IN MY PRESENCE

Why America Needs to Repent for the Kingdom of God is at Hand

"Once we learn who our neighbor is, we are accountable. We are told to love one another. Will the racist then try to convince God that the different skin tone, or hair, or eye configuration still made the person unworthy of love?"

1. The systemic violence inflicted upon people of color is undeniable. How are Christians to address the racism they see in this world?

_____

_____

_____

_____

2. Should the church be responsible for teaching on the subject of racism?

_____

_____

_____

_____

3. The Bible says we are created in the image of God, why do some races feel they are more superior to others.

_____

_____

_____

_____

4. Is racism more detrimental or outlandish than any other sin? Explain.

_____

_____

_____

_____

5. How do racist people use God as a means to support racism?

_____

_____

_____

_____

6. Can a person be a racist and a Christian? Why or why not?

_____

_____

_____

_____

7. How do we justify the term "slave" used in the Biblical text?

_____

_____

_____

_____

8. After studying this chapter, what am I going to do differently?

_____

_____

_____

_____

Chapter 13 – I Repent for

ACCEPTING PROMISCUITY AND ADULTERY IN OUR SOCIETY

Why America Needs to Repent for the Kingdom of God is at Hand

"Sexual sins, promiscuity, and adultery have been with us throughout humanity's history. Like all sin, if humans are present, sin is present also."

1. Why have people become more open to accepting sinful relationships?

    _____

    _____

    _____

    _____

2. Should the church have a doctrinal statement that defines the church's beliefs about human sexual behavior?

    _____

    _____

    _____

    _____

3. What factors have contributed to activities that have led to an increase in behaviors that would be considered sexual idolatry?

_____

_____

_____

_____

4. Is promiscuous behavior an inherited trait passed down from one generation to another? Why or why not?

_____

_____

_____

_____

5. Give an example of a Biblical text from the Old and New Testaments that addresses the subject of promiscuous behavior.

_____

_____

_____

_____

6. How have society's standards changed over the past decade regarding sexual behavior?

_____

_____

_____

_____

7. What is the Christian's role in being more self-conscious about moral behavior and biblical teaching on the subject of the moral attitude of humankind?

_____

_____

_____

_____

8. Are males more likely to commit adultery than females?

_____

_____

_____

_____

9. In what ways does a person that commits adultery step outside of the order of God?

_____

_____

_____

_____

10. What are the long-term effects of promiscuous behavior on the family unit?

_____

_____

_____

_____

11. After studying this chapter, what am I going to do differently?

_____

_____

_____

_____

Chapter 14– I Repent for
FAILING TO CALL SIN, SIN

Why America Needs to Repent for the Kingdom of God is at Hand

*"Christians should be compelled to call sin, sin. Christians must
call sin out in order for us all to be healed."*

1. Why are most people reluctant to call out sin?

    _____

    _____

    _____

    _____

2. Sin is seen in the moral decay of our society. What are the apparent results of society's sinful
    behavior?

    _____

    _____

    _____

    _____

3. If sin entered the world because of Adam's disobedience, why didn't sin leave when Adam died?

    _____

    _____

    _____

    _____

4. What happens when sin is ignored?

_____

_____

_____

_____

5. Romans 6:23, "the wages of sin is death." Explain!

_____

_____

_____

_____

6. When we confess to Christianity and do not call out sin, does that diminish our faith walk to the world?

_____

_____

_____

_____

7. What is the reality of humanity because of the affliction of sin?

_____

_____

_____

_____

8. What is the cure for the sin of this world?

_____

_____

_____

_____

9. After studying this chapter, what am I going to do differently?

_____

_____

_____

_____

Chapter 15 – I Repent for

LYING

Why America Needs to Repent for the Kingdom of God is at Hand

"These six things doth the LORD hate: yea, seven are an abomination unto him: A proud look, a lying tongue, and hands that shed innocent blood, An heart that deviseth wicked imaginations, feet that be swift in running to mischief, A false witness that speaketh lies, and he that that soweth discord among brethren." (Proverbs 6:16-19 KJV).

1. Why is lying so devastating to God's children?

_____

_____

_____

_____

2. What are some of the consequences of lying?

_____

_____

_____

_____

3. What does God's word say about lying?

_____

_____

_____

4. After studying this chapter, what am I going to do differently?

_____

_____

_____

_____

Chapter 16 – I Repent for

ACCEPTING THE LGBTQ LIFESTYLE AS A GOD APPROVED WAY OF LIFE

Why America Needs to Repent for the Kingdom of God is at Hand

"One can hate the sin and still love the sinner."

1. Is the LGBTQ lifestyle the direct result of sin or a genetic birth defect?

   _____

   _____

   _____

   _____

2. When we obey the laws concerning the LGBTQ lifestyle are we supporting their movement?

   _____

   _____

   _____

   _____

3. What is the difference between *Homophobia* and *Heterosexism*?

   _____

   _____

   _____

   _____

4. Give an example whereby Jesus condemned the sin but embraced the sinner.

_____

_____

_____

_____

5. Do man's legal laws challenge God's moral law? If yes, how so?

_____

_____

_____

_____

6. What sins are an abomination to God?

_____

_____

_____

_____

7. Does the sexual orientation of a person prevent, him or her from being a Christian?

_____

_____

_____

_____

8. Should the church embrace the LGBTQ community to show forth the love of Christ? How?

_____

_____

_____

_____

9. After studying this chapter, what am I going to do differently?

_____

_____

_____

_____

Chapter 17 – I Repent for

NOT SPEAKING UP ABOUT SIN AND EVIL

Why America Needs to Repent for the Kingdom of God is at Hand

"Sin today is so ubiquitous that many people do not even notice there is a problem."

1. Why do people have a tendency to avoid speaking out against the evil that is occurring in this world?

_____

_____

_____

_____

2. Why is there so much sin and evilness in the world?

_____

_____

_____

_____

3. If God is sovereign, why does He allow sin to exist?

_____

_____

_____

_____

4. In Ephesians 6:10-17, Apostle Paul refers to our condition in warrior terms. Explain!

_____

_____

_____

_____

5. Why do men and women commit unspeakable acts of evil?

_____

_____

_____

_____

6. Why do we have a duty to speak out against sin and evil?

_____

_____

_____

_____

7. Romans 3:23, tells us that, "all have sinned, and come short of the glory of God" (KJV). Does this mean we will always have some desire to commit sin?

_____

_____

_____

_____

8. Does God view all sin the same?

_____

_____

_____

_____

9. When we speak out against sinful behavior is it considered being judgmental?

_____

_____

_____

_____

10. As Christian believers, why is it more difficult to speak out against sinful behaviors in a public setting?

_____

_____

_____

_____

11. After studying this chapter, what am I going to do differently?

_____

_____

_____

_____

Chapter 18 – I Repent for

CLERGY: PASTOR, BISHOP, PRIEST, PROPHET, EVANGELIST, AND ELDER ABUSE

Why America Needs to Repent for the Kingdom of God is at Hand

"Our clergy today are not given the same responsibility that clergy may have had in the past."

1. How has the perception of clergy changed in our society over the last decade?

_____

_____

_____

_____

2. In what ways are people abusing clergy that are serving the community?

_____

_____

_____

_____

3. Does God look at clergy differently from other men and women?

_____

_____

_____

_____

4. What can we do to reconcile broken relationships between clergy and some members of the congregation?

_____

_____

_____

_____

5. How has social media contributed to the moral downfall of pastors and religious leaders?

_____

_____

_____

_____

6. Research has shown that pastors are trusted less and held in low esteem each year. What effects will this have on the life of the church?

_____

_____

_____

_____

7. After studying this chapter, what am I going to do differently?

_____

_____

_____

_____

Chapter 19 – I Repent for

IGNORING WHAT NATURE REVEALS

Why America Needs to Repent for the Kingdom of God is at Hand

"The same God who designed an enormous whale, a huge elephant, and a giant sequoia tree also designed the octopus, snakes that slither, and birds that fly. Think of how delicate and intricate the design of everything is and how it all has to work together."

1. What lessons can we learn from God's design of nature?

_____

_____

_____

_____

2. What does nature teach us about God?

_____

_____

_____

_____

3. In the Book of Job, how did God use nature to reprimand Job?

_____

_____

_____

_____

4. What four things can we learn from nature?

_____

_____

_____

_____

5. How has God designed nature to maintain our existence on earth?

_____

_____

_____

_____

6. God created us! Explain the creation of man in relation to nature.

_____

_____

_____

_____

7. Psalm 14:1 tells us, "The fool hath said in his heart, there is no God." How does nature prove the existence of God?

_____

_____

_____

_____

8. Being in nature, we can see God's handiwork. How can we feel God's presence in nature?

_____

_____

_____

_____

9. After studying this chapter, what am I going to do differently?

_____

_____

_____

_____

_____

Chapter 20 – I Repent for
NOT PARENTING

Why America Needs to Repent for the Kingdom of God is at Hand

"Parenting is not a perfect science but, it must be attempted with all of the vigor, imagination, and ingenuity that we have."

1. Explain why good parenting does not always guarantee good children.

   _____

   _____

   _____

   _____

2. Why is it important for parents to teach their children their core values?

   _____

   _____

   _____

   _____

3. What does God require of parents?

   _____

   _____

   _____

   _____

4. What should you consider when you are making decisions about your children?

_____

_____

_____

_____

5. What should be the major goal of parents when it comes to parenting?

_____

_____

_____

_____

6. After studying this chapter, what am I going to do differently?

_____

_____

_____

_____

Chapter 21 – I Repent for

WORLDLINESS, FALLING FOR THE HYPE

Why America Needs to Repent for the Kingdom of God is at Hand

"Worldliness is when your main concern becomes, "How can I get in the spotlight?"

1. What are some signs that let us know that we are living a worldly life?

_____

_____

_____

_____

2. How do worldly desires affect our lives?

_____

_____

_____

_____

3. Can one be a friend of the world and a follower of Christ at the same time?

_____

_____

_____

_____

4. Why do people equate successful living (big houses and expensive cars) with a worldly lifestyle?

    _____

    _____

    _____

    _____

5. What does it mean when 2 Corinthians 6:14 says "Be ye not unequally yoked together with unbelievers: for what fellowship hath righteousness with unrighteousness? And what communion hath light with darkness?" (KJV).

    _____

    _____

    _____

    _____

6. What are some desires of people living a worldly lifestyle?

    _____

    _____

    _____

    _____

7. How can Christians enjoy life and have fun without living a worldly life?

    _____

    _____

    _____

    _____

8. Why should we keep our hearts, intentions, and motives in check?

    _____

    _____

    _____

    _____

9. After studying this chapter, what am I going to do differently?

_____

_____

_____

_____

Chapter 22 – I Repent for

NOT REALLY KNOWING WHAT JESUS DID FOR ME

Why America Needs to Repent for the Kingdom of God is at Hand

"What is it that Jesus did not do for humanity?"

1. What sacrifices did Jesus make for sinful humanity?

    _____

    _____

    _____

    _____

2. How does humanity describe Jesus as being fully human and fully divine?

    _____

    _____

    _____

    _____

3. Why was it important for Jesus to come in human form?

    _____

    _____

    _____

    _____

4. 1 Peter 1:19 refers to Jesus as a lamb without a blemish or spot. Explain!

_____

_____

_____

_____

5. Adam was tempted by the serpent in the garden and sinned, what happened when Satan tempted Jesus?

_____

_____

_____

_____

6. How does Jesus identify with God?

_____

_____

_____

_____

7. After studying this chapter, what am I going to do differently?

_____

_____

_____

_____

Chapter 23 – I Repent for
TRYING TO WIN AT ALL COST

Why America Needs to Repent for the Kingdom of God is at Hand

"Winning an argument, for some is more important than getting to the right answer."

1. How does winning at all costs affect our relationships with others?

_____

_____

_____

_____

2. Satan competed against Jesus in the wilderness, how did Jesus defeat him?

_____

_____

_____

_____

3. Apostle Paul said, "Let nothing be done through strife or vainglory; but in lowliness of mind let each esteem other better than themselves." (Philippians 2:3 KJV). Does this mean we should look out for the interest of others first, before considering our own interests? Explain!

_____

_____

_____

_____

4. After studying this chapter, what am I going to do differently?

_____

_____

_____

_____

Chapter 24 – I Repent for
TRYING TO FIND ANSWERS IN ALL THE WRONG PLACES

Why America Needs to Repent for the Kingdom of God is at Hand

"Then said Saul unto his servants, Seek me a woman that hath a familiar spirit, that I may go to her, and enquire of her. And his servants said to him, Behold, there is a woman that hath a familiar spirit at Endor." (1 Samuel 28:7 KJV).

1. Is the Bible the only book we can consult to get answers to life's questions? Why or why not?

_____

_____

_____

_____

2. It has been said that we are living in a time that you need the Bible in one hand and a newspaper in the other hand in order to answer life questions. Do you agree? Why or why not?

_____

_____

_____

_____

3. Why do people feel the need to consult fortunetellers or mediums?

_____

_____

_____

_____

4. Is it sinful to play the lottery or play cards for money?

_____

_____

_____

_____

5. What are some of the wrong places we seek to find answers to our questions?

_____

_____

_____

_____

6. After studying this chapter, what am I going to do differently?

_____

_____

_____

_____

Chapter 25 – I Repent for

Giving Lip Service to My Belief, Work, and Faith in God

Why America Needs to Repent for the Kingdom of God is at Hand

"And when Simon saw that through laying on of the apostles' hands the Holy Ghost was given, he offered them money, Saying, Give me also this power, that on whomever I lay hands, he may receive the Holy Ghost." (Acts 8:18-19 KJV).

1. What does it mean to be truly committed to God?

   _____

   _____

   _____

   _____

2. What does giving lip service to God imply when it comes to serving in the Kingdom of God?

   _____

   _____

   _____

   _____

3. What is a lukewarm Christian?

_____

_____

_____

_____

4. Does working in the church and joining different ministries demonstrate commitment? Why or why not?

_____

_____

_____

_____

5. What are some ways we can demonstrate we are Christians other than attending church service?

_____

_____

_____

_____

6. After studying this chapter, what am I going to do differently?

_____

_____

_____

_____

Chapter 26 – I Repent for

BELIEVING I SERVE A ONE-DIMENSIONAL GOD

Why America Needs to Repent for the Kingdom of God is at Hand

"God that made the world and all things therein, seeing that he is Lord of heaven and earth, dwelleth not in temples made with hands; Neither is worshipped with men's hands, as though he needed any thing, seeing he giveth to all life, and breath and all things." (Acts 17:24-25 KJV).

1. How do we treat God as a one-dimensional God?

   _____

   _____

   _____

   _____

2. We know God as the Creator, however; does He continue to create?

   _____

   _____

   _____

   _____

3. Every good and perfect gift comes from God. Does God only bear good gifts?

_____

_____

_____

_____

4. What are some multi-dimensional manifestations of God?

_____

_____

_____

_____

5. Explain the statement, God is a Triune God.

_____

_____

_____

_____

6. After studying this chapter, what am I going to do differently?

_____

_____

_____

_____

Chapter 27 – I Repent for

NOT SETTING THE ATMOSPHERE

Why America Needs to Repent for the Kingdom of God is at Hand

"The atmosphere is very important in our ability to live Christian lives."

1. How does the atmosphere set the tone in our ability to live as Christians?

     _____

     _____

     _____

     _____

2. How does a negative atmosphere prevent us from sharing the gospel with others?

     _____

     _____

     _____

     _____

3. What can you do in your neighborhood to help foster a positive atmosphere?

     _____

     _____

     _____

     _____

4. Name some ways sin is being normalized in our daily lives?

_____

_____

_____

_____

5. How can we live in an atmosphere of hope and faith regardless of our present circumstances?

_____

_____

_____

_____

6. After studying this chapter, what am I going to do differently?

_____

_____

_____

_____

Chapter 28 – *I Repent for*

ARGUING AND DEBATING

Why America Needs to Repent for the Kingdom of God is at Hand

"Humility and composure are suggested ways for a Christian to settle a disagreement. While this may not be easy, it is a stark contrast to the hundreds of people that wind up hurt, killed, or imprisoned each year after some minor debate leads to raised tempers."

1. What has caused Christian believers to be so contentious among each other in the church?

_____

_____

_____

_____

2. Explain Isaiah 1:18a, "Come now, and let us reason together; saith the Lord; though your sins be as scarlet, they shall be as white as snow."

_____

_____

_____

_____

3. Is arguing and debating considered sinful? If so, why?

    _____

    _____

    _____

    _____

4. In Romans 1:29, the Apostle Paul listed debate as a sinful act. However; he disputed with the Jews in Acts 17:17. Was Paul being true to his words in the book of Romans?

    _____

    _____

    _____

    _____

5. As Christians, should we keep silent and accept what is being told to us without debate?

    _____

    _____

    _____

    _____

6. After studying this chapter, what am I going to do differently?

    _____

    _____

    _____

    _____

Chapter 29 – I Repent for

NOT GIVING STRONG SUPPORT FOR THE DISADVANTAGED AND PERSECUTED

Why America Needs to Repent for the Kingdom of God is at Hand

"Do we care enough to do anything about the situation other people are dealing with every day?"

1. The King James Version of the Bible says "love thy neighbor" in several places. What does that mean?

   _____

   _____

   _____

   _____

2. When you cannot provide a complete rescue for a disadvantaged person is it better to give them a partial handout?

   _____

   _____

   _____

   _____

3. Part of Romans 12:16 says "Be of the same mind one toward another", (KJV). How do we do that?

_____

_____

_____

_____

4. Are we being derelict in our Christian duty when we do not offer to help the disadvantaged when there is a need? If yes, how so?

_____

_____

_____

_____

5. What should be our attitude toward the disadvantaged and persecuted people of this world?

_____

_____

_____

_____

6. What efforts should be made to raise awareness of the needs of the disadvantages and persecution that people are facing?

_____

_____

_____

_____

7. How can the church be a channel of blessing to people who are living in harsh circumstances?

_____

_____

_____

_____

8. How can an individual help to support the disadvantaged and persecuted people in their community?

_____

_____

_____

_____

9. After studying this chapter, what am I going to do differently?

_____

_____

_____

_____

Chapter 30 – I Repent for

NOT THANKING AND APPRECIATING GOD FOR MY TRIALS AND TRIBULATIONS

Why America Needs to Repent for the Kingdom of God is at Hand

"Not that I speak in respect of want: for I have learned, in whatsoever state I am, therewith to be content. I know both how to be abased, and I know how to abound: everywhere and in all things, I am instructed both to be full and to be hungry both to abound and to suffer need. I can do all things through Christ which strengtheneth me." (Philippians 4:11-13 KJV).

1. There are many circumstances that can distract our focus from God, life, trials, and tribulations. Why should we thank God for what we are going through?

    _____

    _____

    _____

    _____

2. How does expectation influence our beliefs?

    _____

    _____

    _____

    _____

3. Is it really possible to give thanks to God during our toughest trials?

_____
_____
_____
_____

4. What are some ways we can give thanks when life is not easy?

_____
_____
_____
_____

5. What does giving thanks with a grateful heart mean to you?

_____
_____
_____
_____

6. What are some blessings that God grants to us that may not feel pleasant?

_____
_____
_____
_____

7. Name three things we should always be thankful for, even in our affliction.

_____
_____
_____
_____

8. What are blessings in disguise?

_____

_____

_____

_____

9. After studying this chapter, what am I going to do differently?

_____

_____

_____

_____

Chapter 31 – I Repent for

CHILD ABUSE AND NEGLECT

Why America Needs to Repent for the Kingdom of God is at Hand

"And they brought young children to him, that he should touch them: and his disciples rebuked those that brought them. But when Jesus saw it, he was much displeased, and said unto them, Suffer the little children to come unto me, and forbid them not: for of such is the kingdom of God."
(Mark 10:13-14 KJV).

1. Why do some family members lack the courage to rescue children from abusive parents?

    _____

    _____

    _____

    _____

2. What are some lifelong effects that children suffer because of abuse and neglect?

    _____

    _____

    _____

    _____

3. Proverbs 13:24 says, *"He that spareth his rod hateth his son: but he that loveth him chasteneth him betimes."* (KJV). Explain this scripture.

_____

_____

_____

_____

4. Give an example of child neglect in the following areas:

   A. Physical Neglect _____

   B. Educational Neglect _____

   C. Emotional Neglect _____

   D. Medical Neglect _____

5. What should be the primary reason for disciplining a child?

_____

_____

_____

_____

6. Is child abuse or neglect always an intentional act to harm a child?

_____

_____

_____

_____

7. After studying this chapter, what am I going to do differently?

_____

_____

_____

_____

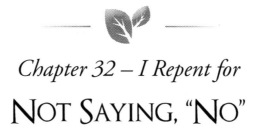

Chapter 32 – I Repent for

NOT SAYING, "NO"

Why America Needs to Repent for the Kingdom of God is at Hand

"Each individual must choose for themselves whether or not it is time to say, "no", and turn around."

1. What makes us not say, "No"?

    _____

    _____

    _____

    _____

2. Does Satan make us commit sinful acts?

    _____

    _____

    _____

    _____

3. How can we know the Holy Spirit from a false spirit?

    _____

    _____

    _____

    _____

4. Explain the verse, "Pride goes before destruction, and an haughty spirit before a fall." (Proverbs 16:18 KJV).

_____

_____

_____

_____

5. Why does it take time and practice to say "No" or set boundaries?

_____

_____

_____

_____

6. After studying this chapter, what am I going to do differently?

_____

_____

_____

_____

Chapter 33 – I Repent for

NOT BELIEVING IN THE POWER OF GOD

Why America Needs to Repent for the Kingdom of God is at Hand

"We should never underestimate the power God demonstrates over the sheep that hear His voice."

1. How would you explain the power of God?

   _____

   _____

   _____

   _____

2. How can we allow God's power to work through us?

   _____

   _____

   _____

   _____

3. What gives us access to the power of God?

   _____

   _____

   _____

   _____

4. Why do most people not believe God is still working miracles today?

_____

_____

_____

_____

5. How do you explain the sovereignty of God?

_____

_____

_____

_____

6. Why do Christians who believe in God say they have not experienced the power of God?

_____

_____

_____

_____

7. Do you have a testimony whereby you experienced God's mighty power in your life?

_____

_____

_____

_____

8. After studying this chapter, what am I going to do differently?

_____

_____

_____

_____

Chapter 34 – I Repent for

DRINKING, DRUGGING, AND GETTING HIGH

Why America Needs to Repent for the Kingdom of God is at Hand

"Alcohol and drug abuse know no boundaries. The richest families to the poorest may be affected."

1. I Peter 5:8 says, *"Be sober, be vigilant; because your adversary the devil, as a roaring lion, walketh about, seeking whom he may devour."* (KJV). Explain!

   _____

   _____

   _____

   _____

2. Is alcohol consumption considered a temptation? Drug addiction?

   _____

   _____

   _____

   _____

3. Does the Bible admonish the use of alcohol and drugs? If so, list any scripture to support your answer.

_____

_____

_____

_____

4. Is drug addiction a disease or a sinful act?

_____

_____

_____

_____

5. Jesus gave wine to His disciples during the last supper. Is wine the only alcoholic drink that is permissible according to the Bible?

_____

_____

_____

_____

6. After studying this chapter, what am I going to do differently?

_____

_____

_____

_____

Chapter 35– I Repent for

NOT HONORING MARRIAGE

Why America Needs to Repent for the Kingdom of God is at Hand

"Marriage is honourable in all, and the bed undefiled: but whoremongers and adulterers God will judge." (Hebrews 13:4 KJV).

1. What is the main reason most couples argue?

   _____

   _____

   _____

   _____

2. How can married couples navigate the hard times in their relationship instead of succumbing to divorce?

   _____

   _____

   _____

   _____

3. What are the benefits of a long-term marriage?

   _____

   _____

   _____

   _____

4. How does divorce impact the lives of the children in the family?

_____

_____

_____

_____

5. What are some fundamental traits of a happy marriage?

_____

_____

_____

_____

6. We are told to honor marriage. What does the word *honor* mean in marriage?

_____

_____

_____

_____

7. What does God's word say about divorce?

_____

_____

_____

_____

8. After studying this chapter, what am I going to do differently?

_____

_____

_____

_____

Chapter 36 – I Repent for

NOT HONORING THE SABBATH DAY

Why America Needs to Repent for the Kingdom of God is at Hand

"And the Lord spake unto Moses, saying, Speak thou also unto the children of Israel, saying, Verily my sabbaths ye shall keep: for it is a sign between me and you throughout your generations; that ye may know that I am the Lord that doth sanctify you. (Exodus 31:12-13 KJV).

1. What is the meaning of the word *Sabbath*?

   _____

   _____

   _____

   _____

2. How should we observe the Sabbath?

   _____

   _____

   _____

   _____

3. The Sabbath day used to be a day of rest whereby stores were closed, and families went to church. Why did this change?

_____

_____

_____

_____

4. What do most Christians find to do with their time besides worship on Sunday?

_____

_____

_____

_____

5. After studying this chapter, what am I going to do differently?

_____

_____

_____

_____

Chapter 37 – I Repent for

WANTING TO BE RICH AND FAMOUS AT ALL COST

Why America Needs to Repent for the Kingdom of God is at Hand

*"Having fame and fortune does not mean a person will be satisfied.
It seems we can never have enough. Even rich people find
themselves not satisfied with what they have."*

1. Why do people seek to be rich and strive to be famous no matter what it costs them?

    _____

    _____

    _____

    _____

2. Is it sinful to be rich or famous?

    _____

    _____

    _____

    _____

3. Has the media encouraged people to aspire to be rich and famous at any cost?

    _____

    _____

    _____

    _____

4. How can the church help shape the attitudes of the members that are materialistic?

    _____

    _____

    _____

    _____

5. Why do you think the story of the rich man that found himself in hell is included in the Bible?

    _____

    _____

    _____

    _____

6. The Bible says, *"For the love of money is the root of all evil: which while some coveted after, they have erred from the faith, and pierced themselves through with many sorrows." (1Timothy 6:10 KJV)*. Explain.

    _____

    _____

    _____

    _____

7. After studying this chapter, what am I going to do differently?

    _____

    _____

    _____

    _____

Chapter 38 – I Repent for

NOT GIVING AS I SHOULD

Why America Needs to Repent for the Kingdom of God is at Hand

"Giving can bring out the best in us and the worst in us because it reveals the heart in us."

1. Why do some Christian believers adhere to the "take care of me first" attitude when it comes to giving to the church?

\
\
\
\

2. Why are people reluctant to give to the church?

\
\
\
\

3. Would members give more if pastors did more teaching on the subject of stewardship?

\
\
\
\

4. Has the megachurch and prosperity preaching added to the distrust of giving to the church?

_____

_____

_____

_____

5. Why should giving always be a personal issue between God and the person that is giving?

_____

_____

_____

_____

6. After studying this chapter, what am I going to do differently?

_____

_____

_____

_____

Chapter 39 – I Repent for
NOT FORGIVING PROPERLY

Why America Needs to Repent for the Kingdom of God is at Hand

"Forgiveness is between you and God, just as much as it is between you and the person that wronged you."

1. How does our willingness to forgive others affect our relationship with God?

    _____

    _____

    _____

    _____

2. What does our forgiveness of others demonstrate about ourselves?

    _____

    _____

    _____

    _____

3. Who benefits more from forgiveness, the one who did wrong or the one who forgives?

    _____

    _____

    _____

    _____

4. How many times should you forgive your sister or brother?

_____

_____

_____

_____

5. What happens to the person who refuses to forgive someone who has done them wrong?

_____

_____

_____

_____

6. After studying this chapter, what am I going to do differently?

_____

_____

_____

_____

Chapter 40 – I Repent for

CELEBRATING SEX APPEAL, SEXUALITY, AND SEXINESS OUTSIDE OF MARRIAGE

Why America Needs to Repent for the Kingdom of God is at Hand

Wherefore God also gave them up to uncleanness through the lusts of their own hearts, to dishonour their own bodies between themselves: Who changed the truth of God into a lie, and worshipped and served the creature more than the Creator, who is blessed for ever. Amen. (Romans 1:24-25 KJV)

1. What is infidelity?

   _____

   _____

   _____

   _____

2. How much has social media contributed to the onset of infidelity in marriages?

   _____

   _____

   _____

   _____

3. How do Christians encourage participation in sexual immorality?

_____

_____

_____

_____

4. Why has the church kept silent when members attend worship service in very provocative clothing?

_____

_____

_____

_____

5. God instructs us to be in the world but not of the world. What does this mean?

_____

_____

_____

_____

6. After studying this chapter, what am I going to do differently?

_____

_____

_____

_____

Chapter 41 – I Repent for

NOT BELIEVING IN THE POWER OF PRAYER

Why America Needs to Repent for the Kingdom of God is at Hand

"Prayer is a method to unleash the power of God. If one believes in His promises then one has to trust His word."

1. How can one develop a consistent prayer life?

    _____

    _____

    _____

    _____

2. Why is prayer such a powerful weapon against the ills of this world?

    _____

    _____

    _____

    _____

3. What did Jesus teach His disciples about prayer?

    _____

    _____

    _____

    _____

4. How many times should we continue to pray for a particular need, if our prayer is not answered?

_____

_____

_____

_____

5. Why should we end our prayer request with, "In Jesus Name"?

_____

_____

_____

_____

6. Will God answer all of our prayers? Explain!

_____

_____

_____

_____

7. What kind of power do we have through prayer?

_____

_____

_____

_____

8. How do we sometimes misuse prayer?

_____

_____

_____

_____

9. What is the connection between praying and fasting?

_____

_____

_____

_____

10. Should we pray in silence or out loud? Give scripture to support your answer.

_____

_____

_____

_____

11. After studying this chapter, what am I going to do differently?

_____

_____

_____

_____

Chapter 42 – I Repent because
GOD SAID SO

Why America Needs to Repent for the Kingdom of God is at Hand

"We are all sinners, saved by grace. All of our righteousness is as filthy rags compared to the awesome holiness of Almighty God."

1. What changes do you need to make in your life to get closer to God?

    _____

    _____

    _____

    _____

2. Why is repentance necessary for us to see God?

    _____

    _____

    _____

    _____

3. What does repentance free us from?

    _____

    _____

    _____

    _____

4. How are we convicted by the Word of God?

_____
_____
_____
_____

5. Can repentance take place without confession?

_____
_____
_____
_____

6. What steps can we take as Christians to change the direction our world seems to be heading?

_____
_____
_____
_____

7. What are some things that the Bible speaks against that have become commonplace in our society?

_____
_____
_____
_____

8. Because Jesus died for our sins, past, present, and future, why do we need to repent?

_____
_____
_____
_____

9. Part of Romans 6:23 tells us, *"the wages of sin is death"* *(KJV)*. How do you interpret this scripture?

_____

_____

_____

_____

For the Kingdom of God is at Hand

Authors

Reverend Jacquelyn B. Jones, currently serves as Director of Christian Education at First Baptist Church, East Martinsville, VA. She is a graduate of Virginia State with a Masters in Media Technology. She is also a graduate of the Samuel DeWitt Proctor School of Theology at Virginia Union University. Rev. Jones resides in Danville, Virginia. She is the mother of two grown sons and six adorable grandchildren.

Pastor Dwane Massenburg earned a degree in Mechanical Engineering from Georgia Tech and a Master of Divinity degree from Virginia Union University's Samuel Dewitt Proctor School of Theology. He's held many church positions including deacon, trustee, youth minister, treasurer, Young Entrepreneurs Club chairperson, Sunday school superintendent, Marriage Ministry chairperson, and associate pastor and senior pastor for three congregations. Massenburg currently pastors Christians United Congregation. He and his wife have three grown children and seven grandchildren

Now that you have read "Why America Needs to Repent" and persistently navigated your way through the questions in this workbook, take a full inventory of what the Holy Spirit has revealed to you. What needs to change? What needs to be investigated further? God is not through with you yet. Stay in prayer. Continue to study.

Share the book with friends. We can change the heart of America by changing the hearts in America, one person at a time. God is real and we have the power to stand up and be counted as Christians.

To receive daily prayers with scriptural content from the author of "Why America Needs to Repent", send an email request to: 1warriorministry@gmail.com. Or, you can follow Pastor Dwane Massenburg on Facebook.

Blessings brothers and sisters in Christ.

ted in the United States
aker & Taylor Publisher Services